Coasts

Kay Barnham

Geography First

Titles in this series
Coasts ● Islands ● Maps and Symbols
Mountains ● Rivers ● Volcanoes

© 2004 White-Thomson Publishing Ltd

Produced for Hodder Wayland by
White-Thomson Publishing Ltd
2/3 St Andrew's Place
Lewes, East Sussex
BN7 1UP

Geography consultant: John Lace, School Adviser
Editor: Katie Orchard
Picture research: Glass Onion Pictures
Designer: Chris Halls at Mind's Eye Design Ltd, Lewes
Artist: Peter Bull

Published in Great Britain in 2004 by Hodder Wayland,
an imprint of Hodder Children's Books.

This paperback edition published in 2006 by Wayland,
an imprint of Hachette Children's Books.

The right of Kay Barnham to be identified as the
author of the work has been asserted by her in
accordance with the Copyright, Designs and
Patents Act 1988.

British Library Cataloguing in Publication Data
Barnham, Kay
  Coasts. - (Geography First)
  1 Coasts - Juvenile literature
  I. Title II. Orchard, Katie
  551.4'58

ISBN-10: 0 7502 4630 8
ISBN-13: 978 0 7502 4630 9

Printed in China

Wayland
An imprint of Hachette Children's Books
338 Euston Road, London NW1 3BH

Cover: Waves crashing on a beach in California, USA.
Title page: Boats moored off a beach in northern Sardinia.
Futher information page: Small fishing boats in Greece.

Acknowledgements:
The author and publisher would like to thank the following for their permission to reproduce the
following photographs: Corbis 15 (Tim Davis), Ecoscene 9 (John Farmar), 16, 18 (Christine Osborne),
23 (Martin Jones), Frank Lane Picture Agency *cover*, Hodder Wayland Picture Library *contents page, chapter
openers* (Gordon Clements), 11 (Jeremy Horner), 13, 22, Oxford Scientific Films 7 (Scott Winer), 12 (Daniel
Valla), 14 (Raymond Blythe), 24 (Steve Littlewood0; Still Pictures 4 (Norbert Wu), 5 (J. J. Alcalay), 17 (R.
Leguen), 20 (Andrew Davies), 25 (Cyril Ruoso-Bios), 26 (Claus Andrews), 27 (Truchet-UNEP), 28 (Al Grillo);
WTPix *title* page, 19, 31.

Words in bold **like this** are explained in the glossary on page 30.

Contents

Coasts and change

A coast is a place where land meets sea. Sandy beaches, towering **cliffs** and sheltered **harbours** are all found on coasts.

The shape of coasts is always changing. Over time, some coasts are worn away, while other coasts are built up by sand and pebbles washed ashore. This can take days, weeks or even hundreds of years.

▼ *This sheltered bay is at Point Lobos, California, USA.*

Most coasts change shape because of the never-ending movement of the sea. Again and again, the **tide** flows in and out and **waves** fall on to the shore.

▲ Jagged rocks jut out along this French coastline.

Powerful waves

A wave is a moving ridge of water. Most waves form when wind blows over the sea – the stronger the wind, the bigger the wave. Waves are also created by the tide. This movement of the sea is caused by the pull of the Moon and the Sun.

Wave Action

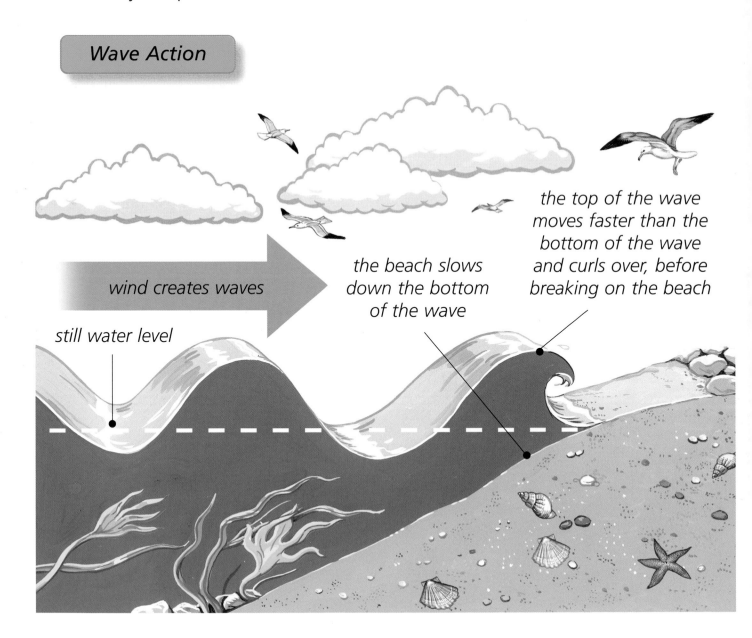

wind creates waves

still water level

the beach slows down the bottom of the wave

the top of the wave moves faster than the bottom of the wave and curls over, before breaking on the beach

Waves can **erode**, or wear away, coasts. The strength of the waves affects how long it takes for this to happen. Crashing **breakers** will erode a coast faster than gentle, lapping waves.

▲ *High waves crash on to the coast of Oahu, Hawaii.*

Headlands and bays

Coasts can be made up of hard or soft rock. Soft rock erodes more quickly than hard rock. Some cliffs are made of areas of hard and soft rock. A bay forms where the softer rock is eroded by waves. Some hard rock may be left sticking out into the sea. This is called a headland.

How Caves, Arches and **Stacks** *are Formed*

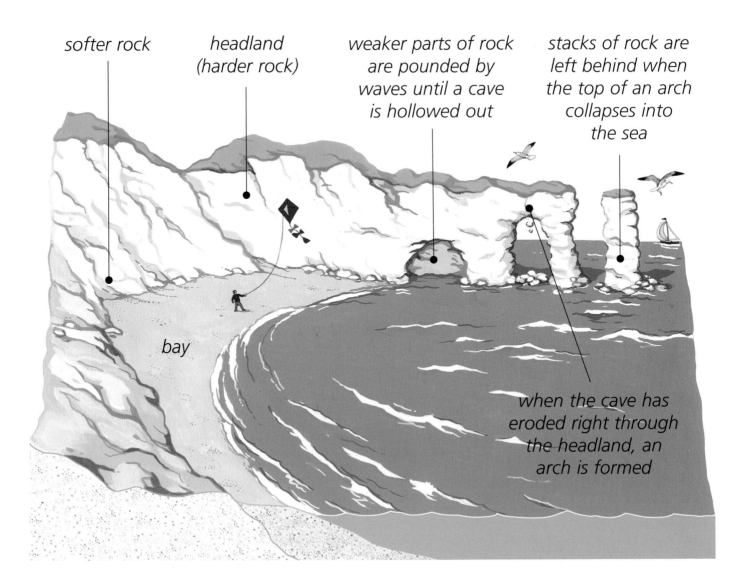

softer rock

headland (harder rock)

weaker parts of rock are pounded by waves until a cave is hollowed out

stacks of rock are left behind when the top of an arch collapses into the sea

bay

when the cave has eroded right through the headland, an arch is formed

Over time, waves wear away the headland itself. Weaker parts of the headland are pounded by the crashing sea. Caves, arches and stacks are carved out from the rock.

▼ *Dorset, UK, has stunning bays and dramatic arches where the sea has eroded headlands.*

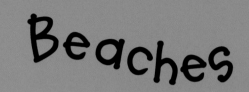

Beaches

Beaches are usually made up of pebbles or sand – ground-up rock that has been tossed ashore by the sea. There are two types of waves. Low, gentle waves carry pebbles and sand up the beach, before the seawater slowly drains away. Large, steep, powerful waves crash on to the beach, then drag this material back into the sea.

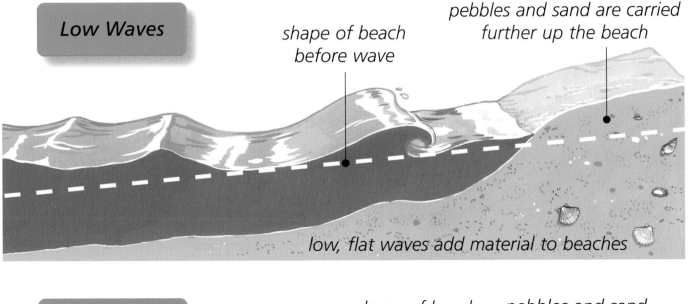

Low Waves

shape of beach before wave

pebbles and sand are carried further up the beach

low, flat waves add material to beaches

Steep Waves

shape of beach before wave

pebbles and sand are dragged back into the sea

steep waves destroy beaches

The top of a beach is the highest place the sea reaches at **high tide**. The bottom of the beach is the furthest the sea goes out at **low tide**.

▲ *A wide, sandy, **tropical** beach in St Lucia.*

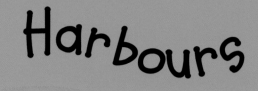

Harbours

Natural harbours are created when waves wear away the coast to form a deep bay. Land on either side shelters the harbour from wind. The water is deep enough to allow boats to sail freely in and out. Big ships, yachts and fishing boats all use harbours.

▼ *Ships and boats can moor safely in this natural harbour, in Majorca, Spain.*

Not all harbours are natural. People build **artificial** harbours, too. Sometimes, a **sea wall** is built near the harbour entrance to protect the ships and boats from stormy water.

▲ *The artificial harbour in Christchurch, New Zealand, is large enough for oil tankers to moor there.*

Unusual coasts

Volcanic islands form when undersea **volcanoes** erupt. Beaches on these islands are often made up of very dark sand. This sand is made from the **lava** that erupted from the volcano. It is heavier than the sand that is usually washed on to beaches.

▼ *This beach in Santorini, Greece, is made up of black volcanic sand.*

Antarctica, the continent at the **South Pole**, is completely covered in ice and snow. It is so cold that the sea around Antarctica freezes over. It is difficult to tell where the coast ends and where the sea begins.

▼ *Penguins live next to the icy sea around Antarctica. They dive into the water to catch fish.*

Coastal wildlife

Coasts are home to a wide range of plants and animals. Seaweeds can survive in and out of the water, carried ashore by the tide. Grasses grow a little further inland. Overhead, seabirds such as gulls and albatrosses swoop and feed, catching fish.

▼ *Puffins nest on a cliff in the Shetland Islands.*

Crabs, starfish and sea snails live in rock pools – holes in the rocks that fill with water when the tide comes in.

Seals, sea otters and sea lions live in the sea. They clamber on to land to find a mate or to give birth to their young.

▲ *Leatherback turtles live in the sea, but lay their eggs on sandy beaches. When the young turtles hatch, they crawl straight to the sea.*

People and coasts

Many people live and work in coastal areas. Some people simply enjoy living beside the sea. Others depend on the sea for work. Fishermen catch fish, which they sell to markets, shops and restaurants.

▼ *Fishermen check their fishing nets in Zanzibar, Tanzania.*

Coastal areas are often beautiful. In summer, wide sandy beaches attract lots of tourists. Hotels, cafés and campsites are built along the seafront to look after these holidaymakers.

However, building in coastal areas can harm the **environment**. Also, if there are too many people around, wildlife can be frightened away.

▼ *Tourist resorts like this one in Australia can be very busy places. New hotels and apartments are built to cope with all the extra people.*

Sea defences

Sometimes, the sea erodes coastal settlements and places of natural beauty. When the sea pounds against cliffs, these can crumble. Waves crash against the shore, carrying away sand, earth and pebbles.

▼ *A sandbank prevents the sea from flooding the flat land of Cardiff Bay, UK.*

lighthouse would be in danger if there was no protection at the foot of the cliff

hard rocks piled up at the base of a cliff

sea hits the rocks rather than the bottom of the cliff

Different sorts of sea defences are used to protect the coast from erosion. Sea walls prevent the sea from **flooding** the land. Rocks placed at the foot of a cliff stop waves from smashing against the cliff itself. However, sea defences can cause problems, pushing waves towards other parts of the coast instead.

New coasts

In some places, there is not enough flat land to build new buildings. Earth, stones and rocks can be pushed into the sea to make new land. This is called **reclaimed** land. Around the world, homes, buildings and even airports are built on reclaimed land. The new coastlines are usually very straight.

▼ *Shatin New Town, Hong Kong, is built on land that has been reclaimed from the sea.*

Some coasts are so low-lying that they are in constant danger of being flooded. **Dykes** (wide walls) are sea defences that are built to stop the sea from flowing over the land. Storm barriers can stop low-lying areas from flooding during rough weather.

▼ *Storm barriers like this one protect the Dutch coast from very rough seas and high tides.*

Dangerous coasts

Many coasts have hidden dangers. Jagged rocks under the water's surface can damage and sink a boat. Strong tides and underwater **currents** (movements of the sea) can quickly drag swimmers into deep water.

▼ Coastguards train regularly to rescue sailors and swimmers who are in danger.

Some coasts are well known for their stormy weather and rough seas. At night and in fog, lighthouses shine bright beams of light out to sea, warning sailors that they are near dangerous coasts. Bright plastic floats called buoys mark a safe route through the rocks, guiding boats back to shore.

▲ *Waves batter a lighthouse in Le Havre, France. These waves could force a boat on to dangerous rocks.*

Rising sea levels

The future of the world's coastlines is under threat. The **atmosphere** (the air around Earth) is slowly getting hotter because of the **pollution** that people produce. This **global warming** could melt some of the ice at the North and South Poles, causing sea levels around the world to rise.

▼ As temperatures become warmer, ice in **polar regions** melts and sea levels rise.

As the sea levels climb, some low-lying coastal areas may be flooded for ever. Many countries are trying to slow down global warming by reducing their pollution levels. New sea defences are planned to protect coasts from the rising sea.

▼ *Beautiful, low-lying islands, like Bora Bora in French Polynesia, are in real danger from rising sea levels.*

Coast fact file

1. Canada is the country with the longest coastline in the world, measuring 243,360 kilometres, including islands.

2. The country with the shortest coastline in the world is Monaco, at 5.6 kilometres.

3. The highest sea cliffs in the world are on the Molokai coast in Hawaii. They are 1,010 metres tall.

4. On 25 March, 1989, the *Exxon Valdez* oil tanker created the worst coastal oil spill (below). About 2,400 kilometres of Alaskan coast were ruined and huge numbers of wildlife wiped out.

5. The highest tide in the world takes place in the Bay of Fundy, New Brunswick, Canada. The tidal range (the height difference between high and low tide) can be as much as 16 metres.

6. The **tidal power station** on the River Rance in Brittany, France, is the only tidal power station in the world. It generates enough power to light up a small town.

7. The largest tidal bore – a wave caused by a tide – was about 9 metres high and 320 kilometres long. It rushed over Hangzhou Bay, China, on 18 August, 1993.

8. The largest natural harbour in the world is Sydney Harbour, Australia.

9. The world's largest artificial harbour was built at Jebel Ali, Dubai, in 1976.

10 Tsunamis are huge waves caused by underwater earthquakes or volcanic eruptions. In 1703, a powerful tsunami hit the coast at Awa, Japan, causing 100,000 deaths.

11 The coastlines of the world measure 1.6 million kilometres in total.

Map of Coast Facts

Alaska
4

Canada
1

5

France
6

2

China

10

Japan

7

9

Australia

8

Numbers on this map refer to numbers in the fact file.

Glossary

Artificial Made by people.

Atmosphere The layer of air around Earth.

Breaker A tall, crashing wave.

Cliff A steep, almost vertical, coastline.

Current Strong, underwater movements of the sea.

Dyke A wide wall made of earth, with water on one side.

Environment The world around us.

Erode Wear away.

Flood When water covers land.

Global warming When the temperature of the air around Earth rises because of high pollution levels.

Harbour A place for ships to moor.

High tide The highest level that the sea reaches at the coast.

Lava Molten rock that flows or shoots out of a volcano.

Low tide The lowest level that the sea reaches at the coast.

Polar regions Areas that are near to the North or South poles.

Pollution Damage to air, water or land caused by harmful materials.

Reclaim To gain something back.

Sea wall A wall built to stop the sea flooding the land.

South Pole The point on the globe that is furthest south.

Stack A tall piece of cliff that remains when the rest is worn away.

Tidal power station A place that turns the power of the tide into energy that can be used by people.

Tide The rise and fall of the sea on the shore, caused by the pull of the Moon and the Sun.

Tropical Places that are hot all year round.

Volcano A mountain with a gap through which lava escapes from under the Earth's surface.

Wave A ridge of water that moves across the sea.

Further information

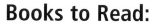

Books to Read:

Bustling Coastlines (The Natural World) by Barbara Taylor (Ticktock Media, 2001)

Coasts (Earth in Danger) by Polly Goodman (Hodder Wayland, 2005)

Life in a... Rockpool on the Seashore by Sally Morgan (Chrysalis, 2004)

Seashore (DK Eyewitness Guides) by Steve Parker (Dorling Kindersley, 2003)

Seaside Holidays (Start-up History) by Stewart Ross (Evans, 2002)

The Water Cycle (Cycles in Nature) by Theresa Greenaway (Hodder Wayland, 2000)

Water Power (Looking at Energy) by Polly Goodman (Hodder Wayland, 2005)

Index

All the numbers in **bold** refer to photographs and illustrations as well as text.